A HEAD START THAT'S A FUN START!

Disney's Read-and-Grow Library makes story time a special time. It's filled with:

- favorite Disney characters;
- colorful stories; and
- important early-learning concepts.

Collect each volume, and create a read-aloud library just right for your growing child.

1   Disney's Mickey's Alphabet Soup
2   Disney's Count on Donald!
3   Disney's Colors, Colors Everywhere!
4   Disney's The Missing Shapes Mix-up
5   Disney's The Amazing Muffin Search
6   Disney's Mickey's World of Words
7   Disney's Telling Time with Goofy
8   Disney's Follow Your Nose, Donald
9   Disney's Goofy Shapes Up
10   Disney's Look Before You Leap!
11   Disney's Minnie's Small Wonders
12   Disney's Daisy's Nature Hunt
13   Disney's Mickey's Weather Machine
14   Disney's Donald Duck Directs
15   Disney's Minnie's Surprise Trip
16   Disney's All in a Day's Work
17   Disney's Uncle Scrooge Comes Home
18   Disney's The Laugh-Along Mystery
19   Disney's Parents' Guide

PARENTS' GUIDE

Published by Advance Publishers
Winter Park, Florida

Written by Lisa Trumbauer   Edited by Bonnie Brook
Illustrated by Megan Montague Cash
Designed by Design Five
Cover art by Peter Emslie
Cover design by Irene Yap

ISBN: 1-885222-94-7
10 9 8 7 6 5 4 3 2 1

Disney's

Disney's — READ and GROW 1
MICKEY'S ALPHABET SOUP

Disney's — READ and GROW 2
COUNT ON DONALD!

18 engaging storybooks that teach while they entertain...

Disney's — READ and GROW 4
THE MISSING SHAPES MIX-UP

Disney's — READ and GROW 5
THE AMAZING MUFFIN SEARCH

Disney's — READ and GROW 3
COLORS, COLORS EVERYWHERE!

Disney's — READ and GROW 9
GOOFY SHAPES UP

Disney's — READ and GROW 6
MICKEY'S WORLD OF WORDS

Disney's — READ and GROW 7
TELLING TIME WITH GOOFY

Disney's — READ and GROW 8
FOLLOW YOUR NOSE, DONALD

Disney's
LOOK BEFORE YOU LEAP!
READ and GROW 10

Disney's
MINNIE'S SMALL WONDERS
READ and GROW 11

Disney's
DAISY'S NATURE HUNT
READ and GROW 12

Disney's
MICKEY'S WEATHER MACHINE
READ and GROW 13

Disney's
DONALD DUCK DIRECTS
READ and GROW 14

Disney's
MINNIE'S SURPRISE TRIP
READ and GROW 15

Disney's
ALL IN A DAY'S WORK
READ and GROW 16

CONSTRUCTION WORKER WANTED
TEACHER WANTED
FIRE-FIGHTER WANTED
POLICE OFFICER WANTED
POSTAL WORKER WANTED

Disney's
UNCLE SCROOGE COMES HOME
READ and GROW 17

Disney's
THE LAUGH-ALONG MYSTERY
READ and GROW 18

Disney's
PARENTS' GUIDE
READ and GROW 19

And this special parents' guide just for *you!*

A Word to Parents about Early Learning

◆ Why Early Learning?

From the moment children are born, they begin to learn about their world. At first they may only take in the sights and sounds of their immediate environment. But soon, they begin to build upon these early impressions, exploring the world around them. As children grow and develop, each new experience becomes an opportunity for learning. Young children want to know everything!

All of this makes early childhood a wonderful time for you to introduce your child to essential early-learning skills. Reading, counting, comparing, telling time—these are basic tools that help children discover the world as they learn and grow. By taking advantage of your child's insatiable curiosity and quest for knowledge, you can help reinforce these necessary early-learning skills, preparing your child for the days of school—and life—ahead.

◆ How Does Disney's Read-and-Grow Library Help with Early Learning?

Everybody loves a good story, especially young children. And when the stories feature fun and familiar characters, children respond even more enthusiastically. That is what makes Disney's Read-and-Grow Library so special. Concepts for early learning—such as reading skills, math skills, comparing and contrasting, visual discrimination, and creative thinking—are presented within the context of stories.

By following the antics of Mickey, Donald, Minnie, Daisy, Goofy, and other beloved Disney characters, children not only laugh along, but also grasp important early-learning concepts as well. Recognizing letters and numbers, distinguishing shapes and colors, understanding safety and good health, and discovering our communities and how they work are just a few of the many early-learning concepts children will uncover within the 18 volumes.

◆ Reading and Language Skills

From the moment your child first utters the words "mama" and "dada," he or she is making the connection between words and objects—and making a connection to you. As more and more words become part of their vocabularies, children begin to form sentences. And the first time children pick up books, they learn that the words they speak can also be words they see. The books in Disney's Read-and-Grow Library strive to make that connection simple and fun. You can share in the process by reading. Children will not only want to hear stories again, but will be encouraged to read the books on their own, as first they develop letter and word recognition, and then put words together in sentences and stories.

◆ Math and Reasoning Skills

Learning how to count is as easy as 1, 2, 3! And it can be fun, too, when children count along with their favorite Disney characters. Early math skills are essential for many other areas of learning. Once children recognize numbers, they can begin to tell time, distinguish shapes, and compare and contrast. Eventually, these skills lead children to more sophisticated levels of thinking, like figuring out why the seasons change and even deciphering riddles. These storybooks follow this natural progression, starting children off with the basics and gradually leading them to higher levels of comprehension.

◆ Critical-Thinking Skills

When children experience new things and acquire new skills, they need ways to organize all they learn. Through reading the stories, children begin to notice similarities and differences, an important skill for comparing and contrasting objects and separating them into categories. For example, children probably learn that a cat, a kitten, a dog, and a puppy are all animals. Soon they will distinguish that kittens and puppies are baby animals, while dogs and cats are adults.

Sequencing is another important critical-thinking skill. Children will learn that letters of the alphabet and numbers follow a particular sequence. Soon they'll realize that the hours of the day follow a certain sequence, as do the days of the week, months of the year, and so on. In fact, even a story follows a pattern, or sequence! As children become familiar with the stories in Disney's Read-and-Grow Library, they'll become adept at categorizing objects and placing them in sequence.

◆ Building Blocks

We don't jump from learning how to count to figuring out intricate math problems. We *build* upon what we learn, piece by piece. The storybooks in Disney's Read-and-Grow Library follow this same principle. For example, in *Mickey's Alphabet Soup* (Vol. 1), children are introduced to letters. *Mickey's World of Words* (Vol. 6) builds upon letter recognition to make common words. And by the time children get to *The Laugh-Along Mystery* (Vol. 18), they are not only putting sentences together, but comprehending what they read!

As the books progress in the series, suggestions are included in this parents' guide for how to use the books as "building blocks," encouraging children to think about the concepts previously learned.

◆ How to Use the *Parents' Guide*

It's easy! This guide follows the same progression as the 18 books in Disney's Read-and-Grow Library. Each book is discussed over two pages. First, you are given a brief overview of the story.

This is followed by a list which highlights the essential early-learning skills the story promotes.

Following the overview are ways to *use* the book with your child. Suggestions are made to enrich the reading experience, including questions that not only help your child comprehend the story but also prompt critical and creative thinking. Ideas are suggested for ways to relate the story to your child's own life, inviting a connection between the story concept and everyday experiences.

After reading the story, you might wonder what else you can do to help your child learn this skill. That's included here, too! Games, art projects, and skill-building activities, all of which make use of materials you have handy around your home, are just a few of the suggested ways to hone early-learning skills.

Children learn best when they can apply newfound knowledge to everyday activities. Learning is not just a school experience. It is a *life* experience. By discussing the stories with your child and trying out some of the suggested activities, you will be helping your young learner toward becoming a *proficient* learner, retaining what he or she learns and applying it to real life. So sit down and embark on a voyage of learning with Mickey, Minnie, their friends, and Disney's Read-and-Grow Library!

What a wonderful way for children to learn their ABCs—making alphabet soup along with Mickey and Minnie! *Mickey's Alphabet Soup* is the perfect way to introduce your child to such early-reading skills as:

- associating letters with their common sounds;

- building a sound vocabulary for reading;

- learning the order of letters in the alphabet;

- recognizing capital and lower-case letters.

Using Mickey's Alphabet Soup

As you share *Mickey's Alphabet Soup* with your child, encourage him to have fun responding to the Disney characters he recognizes and the comical situations he sees. As you read the book the first time, let your child react to the entertaining illustrations. Then read the book again. Point out objects in the pictures that have the same beginning sound. Once your child becomes accustomed to the book, encourage him to find other objects with similar sounds on his own.

Point out the capital and lowercase letters highlighted on each page. Tell your child that even though they may look different, these letters are the same. One is the capital letter, or big letter, and the other is the lowercase

letter, or small letter. Encourage your child to trace the letters with a finger to get a feel for the shape.

The purpose of letters might be a mystery to your child. Explain that each letter has a sound. These are the sounds we make when we speak. Point to the beginning letter that is the focus of each page, stressing the sound.

Then look at the pictures. Help your child name the different objects. Which have the same beginning sound? Can he find other objects on the page that begin with that sound? Also ask your child to look around your home or room. Can he find other objects with that sound?

Read-and-Grow Activities

◆ Learn Your ABCs

Learning the ABCs is a child's first step on the road to reading. Point out to your child that the letters of the alphabet follow a certain order. It is the same order as the letters highlighted on each page of *Mickey's Alphabet Soup*. Practice saying the letters with your child, perhaps introducing him to the traditional ABC song.

◆ Put It All Together— and Read Words!

Recognizing and sounding out beginning letters will also help your child learn to read. Remind your child that the rest of the letters in the words also make sounds. By putting all these sounds together, he can read new words.

Show your child what you mean. Ask your child to choose a favorite illustration in *Mickey's Alphabet Soup*. Then choose one object, and find the written word on the page. If the word is not found in the text, write it on a separate sheet of paper. Sound out each separate letter as you move your finger under the word from left to right, pointing to each letter.

Continue this early-reading process with other stories your child enjoys. As instances come up, point out to your child that some letters can have different sounds. For example, the letter *C* can be hard, as in *cookies*, or soft, as in *cereal*.

◆ Matching Capital and Lowercase Letters

Help your child remember which capital letter goes with each lowercase letter. On the front of 26 separate envelopes, write one capital letter.

Open the flap of the envelope, and on the inside of the flap, write the matching lowercase letter. Then cut out small squares labeled with lowercase letters. Have your child match the letters by placing the small paper squares in the correct envelopes. When he lifts the envelope flap, the lowercase letter will be revealed, providing your child with the correct answer.

◆ Make Your Own Alphabet Soup!

Remind your child that Mickey and Minnie found foods for each letter of the alphabet. Invite your child to flip through magazines to find pictures of foods for each letter, too. Ahead of time, write each letter on a separate index card. As your child finds and cuts out food pictures, instruct him to place the picture next to the card with the same beginning sound. Let your child draw pictures for any letters that still need foods.

◆ Let's Go Shopping!

Go through your kitchen, pointing out letters your child recognizes. Sound out familiar items. For example, he could read the *S* on a can of soup, or the *C* on a box of cookies.

◆ Wrap It Up!

The more your child associates words with the objects they stand for, the closer he gets to becoming a good reader. Keep reading *Mickey's Alphabet Soup* and other books with your child. Watch how much progress he makes!

Mickey needs to collect 20 pinecones for Minnie, and Donald needs to find 20 acorns for Daisy. But Chip and Dale have other ideas! *Count on Donald!* will help your child:

- 🐭 recognize the numerals *1* through *20*;

- 🐭 read the words representing the numbers *one* through *twenty*;

- 🐭 learn the order of numbers;

- 🐭 begin to think about adding and subtracting.

Using Count on Donald!

The first time you read *Count on Donald!* with your child, encourage her to enjoy the antics of Chip and Dale and the joke they play on Mickey and Donald. Then read the book again, and this time, point out how numbers are used. Explain that numbers are important to this story. Can your child tell you why? Guide her to realize that if the characters weren't using numbers, they wouldn't know how many pinecones and acorns they had!

Invite your child to count along with you, from *1* to *20*. Then read the book, and point out that Mickey, Donald, Chip, and Dale are also counting from *1* to *20*. Explain to your child that numbers tell us "how many." For each page, ask your child "how many" acorns or

pinecones she counts. Then help her read the numeral and number word.

As you read, help your child realize that the numbers go in a particular order. Count to *20* with your child. Then read the book and follow the numbers with Mickey and Donald. They count in the same order as you do, don't they? That's because this order never varies.

Invite your child to practice writing numbers. Tell your child to trace the numbers first with her finger. Then provide your child with a thick pencil or crayon, and have her follow the same movements. Watch to make sure your child is holding the pencil correctly, perhaps modeling how to hold it for her.

Read-and-Grow Activities

◆ Adding and Subtracting

As Mickey, Donald, Chip, and Dale count numbers, they are adding and subtracting. Help your child realize this. Each time Mickey finds a pinecone, add the numbers on paper as Mickey adds them in his head. For example, 1 + 1 = 2, 2 + 1 = 3. Guide your child to understand that every time the number *1* is added, the total goes up by one. This is adding.

Likewise, help your child subtract as Dale takes acorns from Donald's basket. For example, 20 − 1 = 19, 19 − 1 = 18, and so on. Explain that as the number *1* is taken away, the total goes down by one. This is subtracting.

You might also read the story in two ways: Read through "Mickey's" story to practice adding. Read through "Donald's" story to practice subtracting.

Make sure your child understands that *1* isn't the only number we can use for adding and subtracting. We can add and subtract all numbers, even those higher than *1*.

◆ Collecting Acorns and Pinecones

Help your child learn to count, add, and subtract by manipulating real items. Before you read, get a box to serve as Donald's basket and a bag to serve as Mickey's sack. Then gather together like objects to be the "acorns" and "pinecones," such as fruit, marshmallows, or toy cars. Or, draw and cut out pictures of 20 individual pinecones and acorns.

Place the items on the table, and reread the book with your child. As the characters find the acorns and pinecones, ask your child to count the items on the table and place them in the bag or box.

◆ Counting with Trees

Mickey and Donald were collecting pinecones and acorns. Remind your child that pinecones and acorns grow on trees. Use tree drawings to help your child count. Draw the outline of an evergreen on a sheet of paper, and cut out drawings of pinecones. You might also draw an oak tree on a separate sheet of paper, along with acorns. Place some pinecones on the evergreen, and challenge your child to count them. Add a pinecone, and ask how many pinecones there are now. As you take away pinecones, ask your child how many pinecones are left. Do the same with the acorns and the oak tree.

◆ Count Around the House

To show your child that counting is an everyday activity, count objects she sees every day. For example, with your child, count the number of books on a shelf, the number of cans in a cabinet, the number of pillows on a couch, and so on. Add or take away one item, and challenge your child to tell you how many you have now.

◆ Wrap It Up!

As your child becomes more familiar and comfortable with numbers, she will enjoy counting along with Mickey and Donald. As you enjoy *Count on Donald!*, point to other items for your child to count, such as trees, leaves, and anything else in the pictures that attracts her.

COLORS, COLORS EVERYWHERE!

Mickey enlists the help of Morty and Ferdie to paint his house, but they're missing certain colors. Or are they? As your child learns how Mickey paints his house, he will:

- identify the colors *red, blue, yellow, black, white, brown, green, purple,* and *orange*;

- discover that mixing colors makes new ones;

- build a vocabulary of color words;

- notice how color adds to the world around us.

Using Colors, Colors Everywhere!

The first time you read the book with your child, invite him to laugh along with Morty, Ferdie, and Goofy as they make a big painted mess. You might ask your child what he thinks Mickey will do when he comes home and sees his house splattered in paint. Will he be happy or sad? React with your child over the clever way Mickey decides to use his paints.

As you read the book again, point to different objects on each page, and challenge your child to identify the color. Ask your child to find and show you other objects on the page that are the same color. For example, point to the red paint. Ask your child, "What color is this?" When he says, "Red," ask, "Do you see other objects on the page that are red, too?"

As your child becomes familiar with the colors, help him discover how certain colors are made. You might introduce the term "primary colors." Explain that red, blue, and yellow are primary colors. Can your child tell you why? Because by mixing them, we can make other colors, including green, orange, and purple!

Conclude by asking your child to take a look around him. His world is full of colors, isn't it? How many different colors can he identify?

Read-and-Grow Activities

◆ Colors of the Rainbow

At the very end of the story, Minnie tells Mickey that his house looks like a rainbow. Share with your child that Minnie was right. Mickey's house does hold most of the rainbow's colors. With your child, make a rainbow collage. On a large sheet of poster board or the white side of wrapping paper, draw a huge rainbow outline, with six bands. Don't add the colors.

Show your child the rainbow. Help him name each color band. Starting at the bottom, write *red*, *orange*, *yellow*, *green*, *blue*, and *purple*. (The rainbow actually has seven bands of color. After blue are indigo and violet. For this activity, purple is fine.) Help your child associate the color word with the color.

Tell your child that together you are going to create a collage of rainbow colors. Flip through old magazines, and cut out pictures for each color. Help your child glue or tape them to the correct color band. When finished, your child will have a rainbow collage to help him remember all the colors he sees.

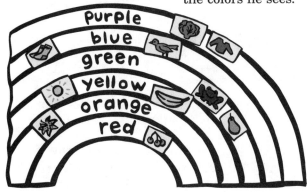

◆ Mix It Up

Let your child experiment with mixing colors. If your child has a paint set, invite him to mix the colors, just as Morty and Ferdie accidentally did, to make pink, gray, green, orange, purple, and brown.

If paints aren't available, let your child try using markers to mix colors. You won't be able to make

pink or gray. However, if your child draws a patch of yellow, then lightly adds blue marker, he'll make green. And if he lightly adds red marker to a yellow patch, he'll make orange! Red and blue markers blended together will create a deep purple!

Invite your child to draw or paint pictures with the new colors. You might make color equations to help your child remember which colors to mix:

- yellow + blue = green
- yellow + red = orange
- red + blue = purple
- red + blue + yellow = brown

◆ Marker Magic

To show your child that the individual primary colors really exist in green, orange, and purple, try this fun experiment. Cut a white coffee filter into three strips. At the bottom of each strip, draw a dot with a colored marker for each one of these colors: orange, green, and purple. Place about an inch of water in three separate paper cups, and attach each strip to the edge with a clothespin, making sure the bottom of the filter touches the water. As the filter absorbs the water and passes through the color, flowing upward, your child will see the color separate into its two primary colors!

◆ Wrap It Up!

Your child will continue to become familiar with colors as he explores his world every day. As your child reads *Colors, Colors Everywhere!* and other Disney books, encourage him to notice the colors and how they add life to the stories.

THE MISSING SHAPES MIX-UP

What happened to all the shapes? That's what Mickey has to find out as triangles, circles, and squares seem to disappear mysteriously. As your child searches along with Mickey in *The Missing Shapes Mix-up*, she will:

- identify different shapes;

- investigate what makes each shape special;

- discover that everything is made up of shapes.

Using The Missing Shapes Mix-up

Read *The Missing Shapes Mix-up* with your child several times. Help your child find all the objects mentioned in the text that are illustrated in the pictures. Can she find all the round fruits? Can she see the brass triangle? How about all the square boxes?

Once your child is familiar with the story and the shapes she sees, point to other objects not mentioned in the text. What shape is a window? What shape are Mickey's ears? What shape is Minnie's table?

Then look around your home to find objects similar to the ones the book characters collected. Are all dollar bills rectangles? Do you have both square books and rectangular

books in your home? Are your buttons round? Can you find any triangles?

Read the story as often as your child likes. You might finish up by pointing out that Morty and Ferdie used all the shapes to make a circus. What could your child do with all these objects?

If your child is already familiar with basic shapes, ask her to explain the difference between a square and a box. Point out that the square is flat and that we can count four sides. A box has volume (three dimensions), and we can count six square sides. Also point out the difference between a circle and a ball.

Read-and-Grow Activities

◆ Shape Safari

Take your child on a shape safari! As you walk through your home, point out objects, asking your child which shape she sees. Keep track of the shapes by starting a shape chart. Under each shape heading, let your child draw pictures of the objects of that shape or write their names, depending on the ability level of your child. Add to your shape chart as you go along your safari, and even afterward, as your child discovers new objects and shapes on her own.

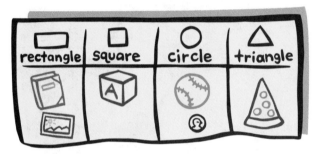

◆ A Shape Grab Bag

Set up a shape grab bag for your child to explore. In a large grocery bag, collect a number of items of various shapes, perhaps taking some ideas from the book. For example, for circles you could include buttons, marbles, small balls; squares could be self-stick pads of paper and computer disks; rectangles could be small books, an eraser, cards; triangles might include an envelope flap, a paper sailboat, a piece of fabric.

Set up four smaller bags. Draw a shape and write the shape's name on each. Then present your child with the grab bag. Challenge your child to grab an object and place it in the proper "shape" bag. Afterward, have your child compare all the objects, confirming that each is the correct shape.

◆ Shape Art

Just as Mickey and Minnie did, invite your child to create pictures using different shapes. With your child, cut out various shapes from construction paper of different colors. (If your child is young, cut the shapes yourself. For older children, make sure they use safety scissors.) On another sheet of paper, encourage your child to arrange the shapes, either making a design she likes or a scene. When your child is happy with her art, help her glue the shapes in place. Be sure to review the names of shapes she used.

◆ Shape Mobile

You can make a simple mobile to help your child remember different shapes. You will need construction paper, safety scissors, tape, string, and a paper plate. Have your child draw and cut out from construction paper a circle, a square, a triangle, a diamond, and a star. Help your child write the shapes' names on the cutouts. Tape a length of string to each cutout. Then tape the other end of the string for each shape around the edge of the plate.

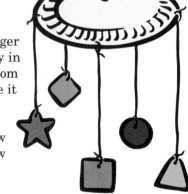

Tape the end of a longer piece of string exactly in the center of the bottom of the plate. Then use it to hang the mobile. Suspend your shape mobile near a window for the shapes to blow in the breeze.

◆ Wrap It Up!

The more you read *The Missing Shapes Mix-up* with your child, the more she will become familiar with the shapes around her. Encourage your child to find new shapes when enjoying the book again.

THE AMAZING MUFFIN SEARCH

What's the difference? After reading *The Amazing Muffin Search*, your child will have no trouble answering that question! As Grandma Duck and Gus try to cook an award-winning muffin, your child will see dozens of similarities and differences. *The Amazing Muffin Search* encourages your child to:

- notice similarities and differences;
- learn how to compare objects;
- identify words that mean the opposite of each other;
- figure out which words have similar meanings.

Using The Amazing Muffin Search

Sit down with your child to laugh along with Grandma Duck, Gus, and Huey, Dewey, and Louie as they try to bake the best muffin, sure to win a prize at the county fair. There's only one problem—Chip and Dale also have their sights set on this delicious treat! As you read, point to certain objects, and ask your child to come up with a describing word for each. For example, you might point to the muffin, and your child will say, "big." Then point to a smaller object for your child to say, "small."

As your child becomes more familiar with the story, challenge him to find the opposites on his own. For example, as Huey, Dewey, and Louie are searching for the muffin, starting on page 26, help your child notice the different

opposites: *up/down*, *near/far*, *high/low*, and *over/under*.

Don't forget to help your child find things that are similar, too. (Help your child understand that similar doesn't mean exactly the same.) You might point out that Huey, Dewey, and Louie are similar, Chip and Dale are similar, and the large muffins are similar.

End by asking your child if he thinks he would like to taste this muffin. Encourage your child to come up with words to describe how the muffin might taste. Will it taste good or bad? What other words can your child think of? Ask your child how the muffin might taste compared to other foods he knows.

Read-and-Grow Activities

◆ Go through the Motions

Come up with some opposites for you and your child to act out. As you say a word, provide an accompanying body movement to show it. Then ask your child to come up with a word that means the opposite, acting out his word, too. For example, you might run in place and say, "Fast!" Your child would then walk in place and say, "Slow!" Or, you could wipe a hand across your forehead and say, "Hot!" Your child should then pretend to shiver and say, "Cold!" Other opposites for this exercise include *big/small, short/tall, happy/sad, sweet/sour, sleeping/awake, heavy/light,* and *push/pull.*

◆ Muffin Match

Write opposite words on slips of paper. Make sure each word has an opposite to match, and that each slip contains one word. Take out a muffin tin. (You could also use an empty egg carton.) With your child, read the words on the slips. Make sure your child knows what the words mean. Then help your child find the slip with the word that means its opposite. When a match has been found, place both slips in a muffin-tin or egg-carton cup. When all the cups are filled, review the words again, talking with your child about how they are opposites.

◆ Let's Play a Word Game

Play a Similar-Word or Opposite-Word game! On separate index cards, write pairs of similar words, such as *big/large, tiny/small.* Do the same for opposite words (*big/small, hot/cold*).

Decide whether you will play the Similar-Word game or Opposite-Word game, and lay those cards

face down on a table. Challenge your child to turn over one card at a time and find its match. Play along with your child, asking him to help you read the words on your cards, too. Each player is only allowed to turn over two cards per turn. When a match is found, the player keeps the cards and gets another try. If a match is not found, the cards are turned back over, and it is the next player's turn. The player with the most matches wins.

◆ You Read My Mind!

Play this fun game with your child to reinforce opposites. Tell your child that you are thinking of something, and supply a description. For example, you could say, "I am thinking of a big animal." Ask your child to draw a picture of what that might be, along with another picture of something that is its opposite. Your child might then draw an elephant and a mouse. At the same time, draw a picture of what you are thinking. The pictures need not be elaborate. Show each other your pictures to see if you came up with the same objects.

Let your child also provide clues. Here are some mind-reading clues to try: "I am thinking of . . . a sweet fruit, a wet place, something soft, something bumpy, a cold food." See how many times you and your child draw the same things!

◆ Wrap It Up!

Our world is filled with many contrasts, yet many things are the same! Each time your child reads *The Amazing Muffin Search,* have him notice a new way something is different or similar.

MICKEY'S WORLD OF WORDS

Everything has a name! And with *Mickey's World of Words*, your child will begin to recognize and read words for a wide variety of objects. This book will help your child:

- 🐭 expand her vocabulary;

- 🐭 develop beginning reading skills;

- 🐭 develop classification skills.

Using Mickey's World of Words

Reading *Mickey's World of Words* with your child is not only an enjoyable experience, but a learning one as well. As your child browses through the pictures and listens to the text, she will begin to learn the names of some common—and some not-so-common—objects. And because the illustrations include labels, she will slowly begin to connect the printed word names with the pictures. Point to these labels and read them with your child.

Every time you read the book, play a different word game with your child. You might tell your child that you see an object on the page that starts with a certain letter (for example, a *B*). Challenge your child to find the object on the page. As you read the label with her,

sound out the word to help her connect the letters she hears with the letters she sees. Also encourage her to apply what she learned in *Mickey's Alphabet Soup* to help read the words.

You could also cover up an object in an illustration, and ask your child to name it by reading the label. Help her by sounding out the letters. When she names the object, reveal the picture to prove she's correct.

Also point out that the objects all fit into specific categories, such as farm items, traffic items, or hardware items. As you turn to each page, ask your child which category she sees. Read the text to confirm the answer.

Read-and-Grow Activities

◆ Mural Labels

Choose a category, such as one of the categories shown in the book, and draw or paint a mural with your child. Roll out a length of wrapping paper on a table, blank side up, and begin to draw. For example, you may choose to draw a street in your neighborhood. When your child is happy with her drawing, help her label the different shops and buildings. You might label them yourself, or let your child practice her handwriting as she writes in object names.

◆ Kitchen Signs

In the grocery store, produce is often labeled with little signs. Have fun making signs with your child. You will need paper and tape. Go through your kitchen, and list some foods your child sees, such as different fruits and vegetables, cans of soup, cereal, and bread. On strips of paper, write the name of a food item. Then tape the paper to the food, or prop the paper next to it. You've made your own mini-market, complete with food signs! It's okay to place the signs inside a cabinet or the refrigerator. When you, your child, or another family member opens the door, the food words can be reviewed.

◆ Grocery List

Every time you write a grocery list, you are naming objects that need to be bought. Next time, ask your child to help you. As you go through the kitchen, bathroom, and other areas of your home, let your child create her own list by drawing pictures of the objects you need. When finished, compare your list with your child's. Help your child connect the picture she drew with the word you wrote. Encourage your child to try to write the word next to her picture, too.

◆ Word File Box

A great way to show your child all the words she has learned is to store her words in an index-card file box. Each time your child learns a new word, invite her to draw and label it on an index card. Then place the card in the box. Words can be stored in alphabetical order. The more cards she has, the more words she's learned!

◆ Family Portrait

Let's not forget that people have names, just like objects! Invite your child to draw a portrait that includes friends and family members. Then help her write each person's name. Sound out the letters as you write them, too. You might create a frame out of construction paper, and display the portrait in your family picture gallery.

◆ Wrap It Up!

Encourage your child to point out familiar words in other books she reads. And as you reread *Mickey's World of Words*, make sure your child identifies and labels other objects in the pictures—even those that don't have labels!

Learning how to tell time is an essential early-learning skill. Most children are aware of time as they keep track of special daily events, such as bedtime and mealtimes. But actually reading the numbers on a clock might be new to your child. *Telling Time with Goofy* encourages your child to:

- recognize the numbers on a clock;
- realize the difference between the big and little hands;
- understand A.M. and P.M.;
- count the minutes and hours between certain times.

Using Telling Time with Goofy

Sit with your child in a comfortable area, and read *Telling Time with Goofy* with him. What is Mickey helping Goofy learn? Tell your child that as you read the book together, you and he are going to help Goofy tell time, too.

During the first few readings, encourage your child to find the clock on the page. Have your child explain how he knows this is a clock. Which features does a clock have? As your child becomes familiar with the story, encourage him not only to find the clock, but to tell you what time it is. You might have a clock nearby so your child can associate the illustrated clock with a clock in your home.

Also talk with your child about why knowing how to tell time is important. If Mickey's nephews didn't know the time, how would they know when to go to school? What did Goofy almost miss because he could not tell time? Talk with your child about special times in your home (for example, the times you wake up, when siblings come home from school, lunchtime, and so on). Conclude with your child that learning to tell time is very important.

Read-and-Grow Activities

◆ Make a Clock

Making a clock for your child to manipulate is easy. You will need a paper plate, a brass fastener, and some paper. First, write the numbers of the clock around the edge of the plate. Then cut out two paper arrows to represent the hands, one short and one long. Poke a brass fastener through the center of the plate, attaching the two paper hands. Your clock is ready to use! (Please note that the brass fastener is not safe around very young children.)

Move the clock's hands to specific times, and challenge your child to tell you the time. Remind your child that the small hand indicates the hour, and the big hand tells the minutes.

Then let your child move the hands as you provide the times. You might choose times from the story (What time was the parade?), or times for important parts of your child's day (When is bedtime?).

Finally, point out to your child that some events have the same hour, even though they occur at different parts of the day. The hour your child eats breakfast and goes to bed might both be 8:00. Remind your child that one time is for morning, or A.M. (midnight to noon). The other is for afternoon and evening, or P.M. (noon to midnight).

◆ Time Schedules

To show your child how important telling time is in his life, keep track of his daily activities by the hour. On a sheet of paper, list the hours

Time	Activity
9:00	eat breakfast
10:00	read with mom
11:00	visit with Sally
12:00	lunchtime

down the left side. As the hours go by, have your child tell you what he did as you write the activity next to the proper hour. At the end of the day, review the time chart with your child, talking about the activities and how time played an important role.

◆ Counting Time

Does your child know how many minutes are in an hour? Or how many hours are in a day? Using the paper-plate clock, review these numbers. Tell your child that during one day, the hour hand of the clock will travel around the clock twice. Have your child count the numbers, then count them again. How many numbers did he count?

Tell your child that the minutes aren't quite as easy to count. Each number on the clock represents five minutes. With your child, draw five short lines for each number around the clock. Starting at the first line to the right of the number 12, begin to count aloud or write the numbers with your child. Your child should discover that 60 minutes make up one hour!

◆ Digital versus Traditional

Remind your child that in the book, Goofy saw two kinds of clocks—a traditional clock with two hands, and a digital clock with numbers only. Help your child tell time with both. Looking at a digital clock, ask your child to read the numbers. Then challenge your child to show the same time using the traditional paper-plate clock. Make sure your child realizes that when it is, say, 8:30, that half of an hour has gone by since 8:00. In how many minutes will it be 9:00? How much of an hour will pass before 9:00?

◆ Wrap It Up!

After you complete these activities, reread *Telling Time with Goofy* with your child. Reinforce the times on the illustrated clocks as your child uses the paper-plate clock to show the hours. Encourage your child to continue to have fun telling time with Goofy!

FOLLOW YOUR NOSE, DONALD

Touching, tasting, smelling, seeing, and hearing are the ways we learn about the world around us. And who better to show children the things they can learn with their five senses than Donald Duck? In *Follow Your Nose, Donald*, your child will discover:

- what the five senses are;

- how to use the five senses to learn about her surroundings;

- why the five senses are important;

- how the five senses help us remember things.

Using **Follow Your Nose, Donald**

Follow Your Nose, Donald is a fun way to make your child aware of her five senses. As you read the story with your child, point out all the things that Donald and his nephews see, hear, smell, taste, and touch. You might ask such guiding questions as: What do you think the waterfall sounds like?; What do you think the sour berries taste like?; and What do you think the pine needles feel like? Challenge your child to compare the things Donald and his nephews see, hear, taste, touch, and smell in the book with things your child sees, hears, tastes, touches, and smells every day.

When you read the book again, point out objects in the pictures. Ask your child to tell you which of the five senses would best help her to learn

about them. You might go through your own home, inviting your child to tell you what she sees, hears, tastes, smells, and touches.

Also, point to the different parts on your body that represent each sense, and ask your child to tell what each does. Reiterate that our eyes help us to see, our nose helps us to smell, our ears help us to hear, our tongue helps us to taste, and our skin helps us to touch and feel.

Finally, talk with your child about how our five senses help keep us safe. For example, our sense of hearing enables us to hear a smoke detector or a warning bell. Our noses help us smell smoke or rotten food. Our eyes help us see flashing lights.

Read-and-Grow Activities

◆ Taste Test

Can your child distinguish one taste from another? Play this game to find out. Ahead of time, gather a selection of healthy foods for your child to taste: for example, an orange slice, an apple slice, peanut butter, a pickle, cheese, granola, raisins, and so on. Then ask your child to close her eyes to taste each one. Can your child guess the food? Write down the answers to check afterward. Point out that even though she couldn't see the food, she could still identify the food by tasting it.

You could continue with similar foods, such as different flavors of ice cream, or different beverages. (Please make sure children don't try this activity with friends. Also caution them never to taste anything that might be harmful to them, such as cleaning products or medicine.)

◆ Touchy-Feely Box

Set up a touchy-feely box for your child to work with. Cut a hole in a medium-sized box, like a shoe box. Place different objects in the box for your child to feel, such as a cotton ball, a toy car, a pencil, a button, a quarter, a tissue. Have your child place a hand inside the box to identify the items. Challenge your child to tell you how the objects feel different. Write down your child's guesses. Then lift the lid and check her answers. Help your child realize that even though the objects could not be seen, her sense of touch helped identify them.

◆ Music to Your Ears

Another fun activity is to see if your child can figure out certain sounds. Ahead of time, collect simple objects that make noise. For example, you could rustle a newspaper, pour a drink, play the radio, slam a book, wind up a toy, turn on a lamp. Even though your child can't see the object, can she guess the sound? Write down her answers. Afterward, confirm your child's ideas, concluding that although she couldn't "see" the noise, she could still tell what it was.

◆ Something Smells Fishy!

Also show your child the importance of our sense of smell. In separate paper bags, place several objects for your child to sniff: for example, an orange, a cinnamon stick, perfume, grass clippings, cookies, a flower, baby powder. See if your child can name the smell without looking in the bag. Again, point out that this experiment is proof that our sense of smell helps us learn about the world around us.

◆ Now It's Time to Follow Your Nose!

Now that your child is aware of all the things the senses do for us, play a scavenger hunt game. Ahead of time, set up a bunch of clues for your child to follow. For example: Look for the big red ball; Move toward the ringing telephone; Where do you smell fresh-baked cookies?; Look for something that feels soft under your feet; and, Where is a tasty, healthy treat? At the last clue, set up a prize for your child to find.

◆ Wrap It Up!

Conclude with your child how our five senses help us to learn about the world. Each time you read *Follow Your Nose, Donald*, have your child look for new ways that the five senses are being used.

Goofy is getting ready for the Scrooge McDuck Marathon Race. But first he has a few things to learn about his body. *Goofy Shapes Up* will help your child:

- identify body parts;

- understand what different body parts do;

- learn ways to keep our bodies healthy.

Using Goofy Shapes Up

The human body is amazing, and your child will enjoy learning how it works as he gets in shape with Goofy. Read the book once for your child to enjoy the story. As you read the book again, identify the body parts Goofy's friends point out, such as the heart, lungs, and muscles.

On subsequent readings, encourage your child to explain the different things these body parts do. Ask your child questions during the reading. (For example, "Do you know what your heart does?")

After your child supplies the answer, read the text to confirm it.

Talk with your child about the different things his body parts help him to do. Do his legs help him to move? How? (Running, leaping, jumping, hopping, strolling, squatting, for example.) What different things can his arms do? (Wave, hug, lift, write, hold.)

Also ask your child if he is aware of the things going on inside his body that he can't see. Can he feel his lungs expand as he breathes in air? Can he feel his heart beat? Does he sometimes hear or feel his stomach grumble? Encourage your child to think about the things his body is doing as you read the book and enjoy these activities.

Read-and-Grow Activities

◆ Body Beautiful

To help your child realize how special his body is, help him draw a life-size body outline on which to label body parts. Roll out a length of wrapping paper, and ask your child to lie down carefully on the plain side. Trace the outline of his body. Then, with your child, label the body parts. Point to the arms, legs, hands, feet, head, chest, and neck. Challenge your child to tell you what each part is called. Help your child write the name of the body part on the paper.

◆ Good to Eat!

Remind your child that Daisy prepared a healthy meal for Goofy to keep his body healthy and strong. If your child is not already familiar with it, review the food pyramid, explaining that doctors have designated certain foods better to eat than others. Keep track of the foods your child eats by drawing a food pyramid for him to fill in. Below is a sample food pyramid of recommended foods.

◆ Exercise Is Excellent!

Reading a book is exercise for your brain. But remind your child that it is also very important to exercise our bodies. Explain that exercise doesn't need to be a formal routine. Playing outdoors is exercising. Swimming with friends is exercising. So are climbing trees, playing tag, and riding bikes. As long as our hearts are beating quickly and our muscles are working, we are exercising!

For one week, keep a record with your child of the different activities he does that could be considered exercise. At the end of the week, talk about the different activities. How did your child feel after completing each one? To remember his fun week, tell your child to draw pictures of the different things he did. Staple the pictures together for your child to have a memento of all the excellent exercises he did.

◆ A Winning Attitude

Remind your child that part of the reason Goofy won the marathon was because he had a winning attitude. He believed he could win. Feeling good about ourselves is very important. To promote your own child's self-confidence, create medals or victory ribbons to recognize your child's special accomplishments and healthy habits. For example, each time your child eats the recommended foods on the food pyramid, help him make a medal to reward himself. Or after exercising with his friends, create a certificate of achievement with your child to reward his good-health practices.

◆ Wrap It Up!

As your child practices good eating habits and healthy exercise, read *Goofy Shapes Up* to compare his healthy routine with Goofy's. And make sure your child doesn't forget that winning attitude!

LOOK BEFORE YOU LEAP!

Keeping safe is probably one of the most important lessons a child can learn. In *Look Before You Leap!*, you and your child will see your favorite Disney characters in some very safe—and some not-so-safe—situations. *Look Before You Leap!* helps your child:

- 🐭 recognize unsafe situations;

- 🐭 learn how to turn an unsafe situation into a safe one;

- 🐭 appreciate the rules that keep us safe.

Using **Look Before You Leap!**

Laugh along with your child as you read the book together. During the first few readings, point out the silly things Goofy, Pluto, and the rest of the gang do during their camping trip.

Reading the book again, point out that these situations are potentially unsafe and only a make-believe or storybook character might get involved in them without getting hurt. As you read, ask your child to identify the unsafe situations (for example, Goofy standing in the street, Pluto hanging his head out the window, Pluto about to jump into the shallow water).

Then ask your child to point out the ways the characters keep safe, such as wearing seat belts in cars, donning life jackets in a boat,

staying a safe distance from a fire, and swimming with a buddy.

Then talk with your child about the things you and she do around the home that keep you both safe, such as not answering the door when a stranger knocks, looking both ways before you cross the street, not playing with matches, and any other safety rules you and your child practice. Help your child understand that all these rules have a purpose—to keep everyone safe.

Read-and-Grow Activities

◆ Neighborhood Walk

Take a walk around your neighborhood with your child, pointing out all the ways people practice staying safe. Let your child find examples, too. Help your child notice children wearing protective gear as they ride bikes or skateboards, drivers and passengers in cars wearing seat belts, cars stopping at stop signs or traffic lights, people walking on sidewalks instead of in the street, construction workers wearing hard hats, and people pausing to look both ways before they cross a street.

When you get home, draw pictures with your child to remember the safety procedures she saw.

◆ Sign Language

Explain to your child that lots of signs are created for safety purposes. Using construction paper, create signs with your child so she can remember them. You could create such signs as a stop sign, a walk/don't-walk sign, a traffic light, a pedestrian crosswalk, a no-trespassing warning, a railroad-crossing warning, a bike-path notice, and so on. Glue the signs to cardboard sticks. Make them stand by forming clay bases or by poking them through a shoe-box lid.

◆ "Say NO to Strangers" Poster

Go to the part in the story in which Morty and Ferdie are approached by a stranger who offers to help them. Why do Morty and Ferdie not accept his help? Stress very strongly that Morty and Ferdie did the right thing: You should never talk to strangers. Explain that the character in this story looked a little suspicious. Sometimes a stranger may even appear nice, offering candy or toys. Make sure your child understands that she should never accept anything from anyone she doesn't know.

Get some large drawing paper, and with your child, draw the stranger from the story. Help your child write across the top of the paper, "Say NO to Strangers." Then draw a big circle with a line through it over the character you've drawn. Help your child hang the poster in her bedroom to remember this very important safety rule.

◆ Safety Rhyme and Reason

With your child, come up with some safety rhymes to help remember safety rules. Children respond well to rhymes, often remembering them for long periods of time. Below are some rhymes to get you started:

- When you want to cross the street,
  Look both ways, then move your feet.

- When you want to ride your bike,
  Wear a helmet. Strap it tight!

Have fun with your child as you come up with these simple, but helpful, rhymes. Test your child by saying the first line, encouraging her to remember the rest.

◆ Wrap It Up!

Following safety rules will eventually come naturally to your child. In the meantime, read books that promote safety, like *Look Before You Leap!,* and others your child enjoys.

MINNIE'S SMALL WONDERS

As Minnie searches for her cherished cat, Fuzzy, she and Mickey come across many different animals and their babies. As your child searches along with Minnie in *Minnie's Small Wonders*, he will learn:

- 🐭 the different names of baby animals;

- 🐭 how animals protect their babies;

- 🐭 which animals are creatures of the night;

- 🐭 the homes different animals might have.

Using Minnie's Small Wonders

Animals and children are a perfect combination. And learning about young animals is especially meaningful. As you share the book with your child the first time, encourage him to hunt through the illustrations with Mickey and Minnie as they search for Fuzzy. Invite your child to point out the different animals he sees, helping him name each one. Also encourage your child to compare the baby and adult animals. How do they differ? How are they the same? How are adult people different from children?

Also guide your child to notice where the animals live. Which animals live in the forest? Which are farm animals? Has your child ever seen any of these animals in real life? What did

they look like? How big were they compared to your child?

The sounds animals make are also enjoyable for children. On subsequent readings, invite your child to provide sound effects, making the sounds of the animals. For example, your child could *moo* like the cow, *oink* like the pig, and *baa* like the sheep.

However, what children probably find most intriguing about animals and their babies is how they live. Share with your child any information you might know about how animals take care of their babies, the things they eat, and the homes they build. Point out pictures of baby animals in books and magazines.

Read-and-Grow Activities

◆ Baby Animal Puzzles

With your child, create baby animal puzzles to put together. On the left side of an index card, draw and label the adult animal. On the right side, draw and label the baby animal. Next, cut the cards apart using different-shaped cuts: for example, a jagged cut, a wavy cut, or a square cut. Mix up the cut cards, and challenge your child to match the baby animal with its parent. If the match is correct, the card halves will fit together, like pieces of a puzzle.

◆ Real-Life Animals

Of course, the best way for children to learn about animals and their babies is to see animals up close. Check around your area for a local petting zoo, or perhaps even a farm that would permit children as visitors. Invite the farmer or zoo guide to talk about the animals and how they care for their babies. Whenever possible, let your child pet the animals, remarking on the feel of their fur or skin. (As Mickey taught Morty and Ferdie in *Look Before You Leap!*, children should wash their hands after petting animals.) Encourage your child to express his enthusiasm for the baby animals he sees. You might bring along a camera to record the moment.

◆ Animal Masks

Act out being animals and their babies. On two paper plates, draw the face of an adult animal, and then the face of its baby. You've made masks! Using the masks, have a conversation with your child about what it would be like to be that animal, living in a forest or on a farm. For added fun, let your child be the adult animal while you role-play the baby. What does your child think the responsibility of the adult animal should be?

◆ Animal Collage Poster

Let your child create an animal collage poster. With your child, flip through old magazines to find pictures of animals. Help your child cut them out. Lay the animal cutouts on a large sheet of paper. When your child is happy with the design the cutouts make, assist in gluing them down. As you work, talk with your child about the different animals he sees. Display your child's animal collage poster on a wall.

◆ Walk Like the Animals

Play an animal guessing game with your child! Take turns pretending to be different animals, making the noises and mimicking the animals' behaviors. Challenge yourself and your child to guess the animal the other person is portraying.

◆ Wrap It Up!

Review with your child all the animals and baby animals he saw in the book. Remind your child that he isn't the only one who is young and depends on a parent or adult. Baby animals all over the world need their parents, too, just the way he does.

DAISY'S NATURE HUNT

L et's go exploring! In *Daisy's Nature Hunt,* your child will explore the outdoors, looking for animals and insects and learning how they interact with the world around them. In *Daisy's Nature Hunt,* your child will:

- recognize common animals and insects;

- identify some common plants;

- investigate how animals and plants depend on one another;

- be made aware of the plants and animals around her.

Using Daisy's Nature Hunt

Get your child ready for a backyard safari! Read the book several times, inviting your child to explore along with Huey, Dewey, and Louie as they try to solve the nature clues and search for the wildlife around them. As you read, encourage your child to think about similar plants and animals she has seen. Has your child ever seen a spider in its web? Or held a ladybug? Or watched a squirrel or chipmunk forage for nuts?

Also point out how plants and animals depend on one another. How do squirrels depend on trees? (For food, like nuts, and for shelter.) How might a spider be helpful to the tree? (By catching insects in its web that might eat tree leaves.) What other examples can children

find that show how plants and animals depend on one another?

Now look around your home for evidence of plants and animals. Did your child know that apples grow on trees? Which other fruits grow on trees? (Oranges, peaches, cherries, for example.) Perhaps you have a fish aquarium, or pots of flowers. Overhanging roof eaves might even boast spiderwebs that you can see from inside!

Read-and-Grow Activities

◆ Your Own Nature Hunt

Even if you live in a city, evidence of plants and animals isn't hard to find. Take your child outdoors to hunt for plants and animals, just as Donald's nephews did. You might bring along the book to compare the things you find with the pictures.

A good place to start is right outside your door or in a park. Take a close look at the sidewalk. You might see ants, spiders, or other creatures scurrying there. Poking around in the grass might also reveal wildlife, including worms and more insects. Checking the branches of trees might reveal birds and squirrels. Remind your child that animals are often afraid of people. If your child tries to stay very quiet, she might see more animals.

On your nature hunt, help your child discover how plants and animals depend on one another. Worms like to eat dead leaves. Dead leaves provide minerals that enrich soil. When the worm pulls the leaf underground, it also brings in these minerals, which the tree's roots then soak up! So the tree provides food for the worm, and the worm provides important minerals for the tree!

To make your walk more meaningful, let your child bring along a pad of paper and some crayons. Sit quietly on a blanket, and point out the different plants and animals you see for your child to draw. Help your child label the picture, too.

◆ Let's Get Growing!

A wonderful way to learn about plants is to grow some. Take your child to a local garden or hardware store to purchase seeds. Let your child choose the seeds to plant. You might steer her toward easy-to-grow flowers (marigolds and zinnias) or vegetables (radishes and leaf lettuce).

Most plants can easily be started with a minimum of soil in a small pot or even a paper cup. Read the seed packet with your child for specific instructions. As your plants grow, make sure your child keeps them watered and in a sunny area.

If possible, you might transfer your plants outdoors. Or keep them on a sunny windowsill in flower boxes for everyone to enjoy. If outdoors, have your child notice insects that come to visit the plants. How do the plants help the insects? How might the insects help the plants?

◆ For the Birds!

Make a simple bird feeder to hang outside a window. Using an empty plastic gallon jug, cut a large hole near the top, big enough for a bird to fit through. You might leave a ledge of plastic for the bird to stand on. Then fill the jug with bird seed, and tie some string around the handle to attach it to a post or tree branch.

◆ Wrap It Up!

Exploring nature and the outdoors is always fun and rewarding. Reading *Daisy's Nature Hunt* with your child before you embark on an outdoor excursion is a great way to prepare your child for the things she might see!

So many amazing things happen in each season that it's hard to observe them all at once. But not if you take a ride in *Mickey's Weather Machine!* As your child travels along, he will:

- learn to identify the seasons;

- learn what makes each season special;

- understand why we have seasons;

- compare the different seasons.

Using Mickey's Weather Machine

Start reading the book with your child. Pause after you read about the snowstorm. Ask your child which season usually has snow. After your child says "winter," continue reading the book all the way through. Encourage your child to respond to the pictures and the fun seasonal things he sees.

Upon reading the book again, spend some time with your child, explaining how the seasons occur. Ask your child if he knew that the earth traveled around the sun. Explain that it takes one full year for the earth to move around the sun.

Talk with your child about the different seasons he sees in the pictures. What does he like best about each season? What does he like to do during this time of year? Which holidays does he associate with each season? Which season is his favorite? Why?

Finally, you might tell your child that not every place on the planet experiences dramatic changes of the seasons. The places that are closer to the equator don't normally have winter. And the places closer to the North and South Poles don't have very warm summers. What is your area like?

Read-and-Grow Activities

◆ Rock Around the Sun

Explanations of how seasons occur might be hard for your child to understand without being able to visualize them. Help your child to do so with this simple demonstration. You will need a globe tilted on its axis and a lamp with the light bulb exposed.

First, acquaint your child with the globe, reviewing that it represents the earth. Help your child find where you live on the globe. Next explain that the lamp is like the sun.

Now have your child notice that the globe is slightly tilted in relation to the pretend sun. Explain that in space, the earth is slightly tilted toward the sun, too. Show your child which portion of the globe is tilted toward the pretend sun. Is it the top portion (Northern Hemisphere) or the bottom portion (Southern Hemisphere)? Guide your child to understand that the portion that is tilted toward the sun is having summer. Which season would the other portion be experiencing? (Winter.)

Now pick up the globe and move it to the other side of the "sun." Is the top or the bottom of the globe closer to the "sun" now? Help your child realize that as the earth moves around the sun, the seasons change.

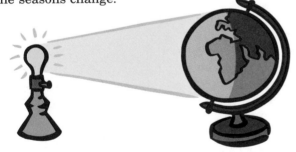

◆ A Book of Seasons

Invite your child to create a book of seasons. Give him four sheets of drawing paper. On each sheet, have him draw one picture to represent each season. Encourage him to think about how the trees change with the seasons. What do the animals do during each season? How about the

farmers with their crops? What does your child do? As your child draws, create a book cover with an appropriate title, such as "How the Seasons Change," or "The Changing Seasons." For younger children, staple or bind the four drawings and the cover together. For older children, suggest that they create one book of drawings for each season. After sharing the books with other family members and friends, keep the books on your child's bookshelf.

◆ Animal Dreams

Remind your child that Mickey told his nephews that many animals sleep during the winter, when food is hard to find. That's a long time! What does your child imagine these animals might dream about? Invite your child to draw a picture of an animal's dream. To practice writing skills, help your child write a title for his picture, such as, "In the winter, the bear dreams about . . . "

◆ Season Chart

Which items does your child associate with each season? Create a chart with four headings, one for each season, and give your child magazines to cut up. Flip through the magazines with your child to find pictures that might represent each season (for example, baby animals and rainy days for spring, apples and changing leaves for fall, warm coats and snow for winter, green grass and outdoor activities for summer). Help your child cut out the pictures and glue them in the appropriate seasonal columns.

◆ Wrap It Up!

Exploring the seasons is exploring the world around us. Each time your child reads *Mickey's Weather Machine*, encourage him to learn and make new discoveries about each season.

DONALD DUCK DIRECTS

People communicate in many different and wonderful ways. Donald Duck is about to explore some of these different forms of communication as he makes a movie about his Uncle Scrooge. As your child reads *Donald Duck Directs*, she will:

- discover how technology contributes to the different ways people communicate;

- identify common forms of communication;

- understand why communicating is important.

Using Donald Duck Directs

Scrooge McDuck wants a movie to be made about his life. And he has assigned Donald Duck the challenging task of producing it! As you read the book with your child, encourage her to marvel along with you at some of the technological communication devices Donald orders, such as a fax machine and video camera. Invite your child to share her own experiences with these things.

Explain to your child that communication is about conveying information to someone else. It doesn't always involve technology—talking to a friend is communicating. Look up "communication" in the dictionary and discuss its meaning with your child. Note that the dictionary helps you communicate the meaning

of unfamiliar words. Ask your child how she communicates with friends or family members who are far away. Help your child understand that people communicate in all sorts of ways. Ask her if she can explain how *Donald Duck Directs* and other books are also a form of communication.

Talk about how machines help us to communicate. What does a fax machine communicate? (Still pictures and writing.) What does a video communicate? (Moving pictures and sound.) What other devices can your child name that help people communicate? Help her understand that the telephone, a computer, a radio, and even a television are all means by which people communicate thoughts and ideas.

Read-and-Grow Activities

◆ We Communicate through Sounds

When we speak, we make sounds. A radio and a television communicate information by sound. Some sounds communicate warnings, like smoke detectors and fire-truck sirens. A ringing telephone communicates that someone is trying to call us.

Sometimes, though, sounds might get misunderstood. This makes communicating difficult! Play a game of "telephone" with your child, her friends, and other family members. Form a line. Whisper a silly message to your child, and instruct her to whisper the sentence to the person next to her, and so on down the line. Invite the last person in line to repeat the message. Is it the same, or has it become garbled? Conclude that when communicating by sounds, it is important that we listen closely. We don't want to miss anything!

◆ We Communicate through Body Language

Ask your child how she would know if you were happy, even if you didn't tell her so. By your body movements! Our facial expressions and body movements communicate all kinds of things! Play a game of "feeling charades." Using facial expressions and body movements only, challenge each other to figure out emotions, such as *happy*, *sad*, and *scared*.

◆ We Communicate through Pictures

Share with your child that we can also communicate ideas and information through pictures.

Flip through a magazine or picture book with your child to study photographs and illustrations. What information can we learn from pictures?

Now let your child try it. Explain that she is going to tell a parent, sibling, or other family member all about her day—using pictures. Invite your child to draw the things she did, then to present the family member with the pictures.

◆ We Communicate through Writing

Share the daily mail with your child. Which type of communication is this? Help your child create a card for a special friend or family member. As you deliver the card, remind your child that writing and sending letters is a way of communicating.

◆ Let's Put It All Together!

Challenge your child to tell you if she can think of an object that communicates with her on many different levels—where she not only sees writing, pictures, and body movements, but also hears sounds. It's the television! Invite your child to put on a television show for you to enjoy, communicating through sound, body movements, and expressions.

◆ Wrap It Up!

Look for ways people communicate—with and without technology—as you reread *Donald Duck Directs* and other books your child enjoys. Remember—reading books may be one of the most fun ways to communicate. It's also a form of communication your child will enjoy for years to come!

Traveling around the world can be fun. But traveling in different kinds of transportation is even better! As he reads *Minnie's Surprise Trip*, your child will:

- identify different kinds of transportation;

- learn how different forms of transportation work;

- understand that we can travel by land, by sea, and by air.

Using Minnie's Surprise Trip

Flying, riding, and boating—these are just a few of the exciting adventures awaiting your child as you get ready to set sail with Mickey and Minnie on their voyage around the world. Read the story with your child. Encourage him to enjoy the places Mickey and Minnie explore along with you.

When you read the book again, challenge your child to identify the mode of transportation he sees on the page before you read. Talk with your child about where Mickey and Minnie are going on this type of transportation. What are they about to see?

Help your child realize that the type of transportation one would find in an area reflects

what that area is like. Would you find dog sleds in Africa? Why are they perfect for Iceland? Would you find sailboats in the deserts of Australia? Why are they perfect for the coast? Recall with your child what he learned about the weather in *Mickey's Weather Machine*. How might weather affect the vehicle you might use?

Talk with your child about the types of transportation he has used. Which means of transportation from the book has he experienced? What was each one like? Which would he like to ride, fly, or boat in? Ask him if he thinks he might like to fly in a rocket ship, like the ones Mickey and Minnie saw at the space center. What a fun trip that would be!

Read-and-Grow Activities

◆ By Land, Sea, or Air?

Transportation can be divided into three categories—modes that go on land, modes that go on water, and modes that go in the air. Help your child make these distinctions.

First, help your child draw three pictures: one for a land vehicle, such as a car; one for an air vehicle, such as an airplane; and one for a water vehicle, such as a boat.

Now help your child write as many different types of transportation as he can think of in the appropriate drawing. Talk with your child about how each vehicle is perfectly made to travel on land, on water, or in the air.

◆ Making Vehicles

Shoe boxes can be used to make all kinds of fun vehicles! Go through the book, and invite your child to choose some vehicles that he especially likes. Then help

him transform a shoe box into a train, a car, a boat, or even a rocket! You will probably need some other art scraps, like construction paper, yarn, stickers, glitter, cast-off fabric, cardboard tubes from paper towels, and so on. Encourage your child to be as creative as possible. When the project is complete, invite your child to tell you where he might go in his new vehicle.

◆ Field Trip Time!

You don't need to go far for your child to see different types of transportation in action. Take your child for a walk around your neighborhood to notice different cars, bicycles, trucks, vans, and so on. Then, if possible, take your child to a station to view more exotic vehicles. A local bus or train station, boat dock, and even an airport are great places for children to explore with you. You might call ahead and try to arrange for your child to have a special tour of an engine room or the cockpit of a plane! Back home, sit down and help your child draw pictures of all the exciting transportation vehicles he saw.

◆ Transportation Mobile

Create a transportation mobile with your child to help him remember the different, fun vehicles he saw in the book or on your field trip. Encourage your child to draw pictures of vehicles and to cut them out. Then help your child tape a length of yarn to each. Tie the yarn to a hanger. Display the mobile in your child's room for him to see the vehicles as they move around on their strings.

◆ Wrap It Up!

Encourage your child to read *Minnie's Surprise Trip* often to learn about the different ways people get around. Ask him to point out to you any new things he notices about transportation each time he enjoys the book. Which other places or vehicles does your child think would be fun to experience someday?

ommunity workers are all around us. *All in a Day's Work* will introduce your child to the very important things community workers do and how everyone pulls together to make a community work. *All in a Day's Work* will help your child:

- recognize and identify community workers;

- develop an awareness of what people do at their jobs;

- foster an appreciation for the hard work people do;

- begin to think about future jobs.

Using All in a Day's Work

As you read through *All in a Day's Work* with your child, point out the various jobs Donald tries. Read the book several times, encouraging your child to laugh along with you at the silly mishaps Donald has. Trying a new job isn't always easy, is it? Help your child understand that often workers go through special training to be able to perform their jobs safely and properly. (This makes a great follow-up to the safety lessons in *Look Before You Leap!*)

After several readings, ask your child to identify the workers she sees on each page before you read the text. For clues, help your child notice the equipment or uniforms the worker might use. As your child names the job,

talk about the different ways this job contributes to a community. What does your child think your community would be like without this worker?

Ask your child if she thinks that she has a job. Of course she does! She is part of a family, just like workers are part of a community. Talk with her about the special jobs she might do around your home: for example, cleaning up her room, helping set the table, watching a younger sibling, or caring for a pet. Also tell your child that she has one more very important job—the job of bringing happiness to the family! (This makes a great follow-up to the plant-and-animal interdependency lessons in *Daisy's Nature Hunt.*)

Read-and-Grow Activities

◆ Observe Your Community

A quick drive or walk through your community can show your child all the different jobs and workers around her. If possible, you might bring along an instant camera to record and remember your trip.

As you walk or drive, point out the community workers you see. For example:

- sanitation workers collecting trash;
- a mail carrier delivering the mail;
- a teacher in a school yard with a class;
- a police officer giving someone directions;
- construction workers erecting a building.

Help your child realize that community workers are everywhere! They are the backbone of any community, working together to make it a better place to live. You might ask your child what the community would be like without one of these workers.

◆ Make a Book of Community Workers

Staple a stack of writing paper or drawing paper together. Tell your child that you have made a blank book for her to draw in. The book is about community helpers. With your child, draw a cover for the book. Then encourage your child to draw a picture of a different community worker on each page. Help your child write the name of the community worker underneath.

◆ Community Worker Role-Play

Which community worker does your child find most exciting or interesting? Encourage your child to role-play that community worker. Your child could be a librarian, helping you check out books. Or you and your child could be construction workers, using blocks to erect a new building. Your child could also be a veterinarian, examining a "sick" stuffed animal. Allow your child's imagination to run free as she role-plays different community workers.

◆ Jobs at Home

Remind your child that jobs are found not just in the community. Working to maintain a home is also a job, a very big and important one. With your child, make a list of the jobs you and your child do at home. For example, vacuuming the carpet is a job. Cooking meals is a job. And taking care of each other is a job. Make a list of these and other household jobs. Each time you and your child complete a job, ask your child to check it off. Which household job does your child enjoy most?

◆ Wrap It Up!

By reading *All in a Day's Work* and observing her own community, your child has been exposed to numerous jobs that make a community function. Continue to point out community jobs and workers as you read this and other stories.

UNCLE SCROOGE COMES HOME

Uncle Scrooge is back from his trip around the world, but he doesn't remember much about it—until he begins to unpack his suitcase. With *Uncle Scrooge Comes Home*, your child will:

- understand that people live all over the world;
- develop an appreciation for what makes people special;
- discover different costumes and customs;
- appreciate his own family and traditions.

Using Uncle Scrooge Comes Home

Get your child ready to embark on a trip around the world with Uncle Scrooge! Before reading the book, ask your child if he thinks people around the world celebrate holidays the same way you do. Then explain that Uncle Scrooge has seen some different holidays, and he's about to share them with his friends.

Now read *Uncle Scrooge Comes Home* with your child. Encourage him to have fun as he learns about the different celebrations Uncle Scrooge experienced. Enjoy the colorful costumes and souvenirs in the book. Point out the things you find interesting and exciting.

Also as you read, review with your child the things he learned about the weather in

Mickey's Weather Machine. How does weather change around the world? In *Minnie's Surprise Trip*, your child was introduced to various ways of getting around. How might Uncle Scrooge have traveled from place to place?

The more you read the book, the more your child will come to appreciate the wonderful differences among peoples all over the globe. Explain that although people might celebrate different holidays and wear clothing unfamiliar to us, there are many things we do share. We all work hard and we all love to play. We all have holidays that are special to us. And we all have family and friends whom we love. In fact, we are all neighbors on this great big planet.

Read-and-Grow Activities

◆ Where in the World?

Uncle Scrooge certainly visited some interesting places! But where in the world are they? Now is the perfect time to have a mini-geography lesson with your child. Pull out an atlas or a map of the world. Can your child show you where you live? Draw an *X* on a self-stick note, and place it on your state.

Now help your child find the fascinating countries Uncle Scrooge visited. You might write Uncle Scrooge's name on self-stick notes for your child to place on each location. Conclude with your child that Uncle Scrooge certainly got around, didn't he?

◆ Simple Souvenirs

To help your child remember the story, make some of the same souvenirs Uncle Scrooge brought home. Here are some simple art projects:

Colored Eggs. Uncle Scrooge brought back decorative eggs from the Ukraine in Eastern Europe. Hard-boil some eggs, then encourage your child to decorate them with markers or paints. You might also visit a hobby shop to buy an egg-decorating kit.

Boats Afloat. In Venice, Uncle Scrooge learned that many people travel the canals in long, thin boats called gondolas. Using the pictures in the book as models, help your child mold gondolas out of foil. Then place them in a bowl of water and watch them float! You might make a cutout of Uncle Scrooge for your child to place in the boat. Pretend Uncle Scrooge is back in Venice!

Piñatas. Uncle Scrooge brought back a piñata from Mexico. Try making this simple one with your child. Take two paper plates and face them toward each other. Staple them along the edges, leaving an open space at the top. Fill the inside with tiny wrapped candies, then staple the plates closed. Have your child draw pictures on the plates, then staple a length of string to the top.

Hang the piñata from a tree branch outdoors, and let your child use the piñata with friends. Standing to one side, challenge children to take turns throwing rubber balls at the paper-plate piñata until it breaks open or falls from the tree.

◆ Explore Your Own Traditions

Every family has its own traditions and cultures to explore. Talk with your child about any traditional holidays you might have celebrated. Compare the holidays with holidays your child knows. With your child, make holiday cards to mark one of your family traditions.

◆ Cooking with Culture

Although he might not realize it, your child probably eats many foods that are eaten in different parts of the world. Start an international cookbook with your child. Don't forget to share and perhaps prepare a food from your own culture for your child to try.

◆ Wrap It Up!

Each time you read *Uncle Scrooge Comes Home* with your child, encourage him to learn something new about the places Uncle Scrooge visited. Compare the places Uncle Scrooge has been with exotic settings and locations children read about in other books.

THE LAUGH-ALONG MYSTERY

Oh, no! Minnie's picnic basket is missing! Will solving the riddles help her find it? Mickey thinks it will! As your child reads *The Laugh-Along Mystery,* she will:

- appreciate wordplay and words that sound similar;

- understand that some words can have several meanings;

- build her vocabulary;

- develop visual and auditory skills.

Using The Laugh-Along Mystery

Children love riddles! Riddles pique children's natural curiosity. And although riddles may seem frivolous, they actually help build important skills, such as language, visual, and auditory discrimination! Have fun with your child as you read *The Laugh-Along Mystery* for the first time. You don't need to ask your child to solve the riddles yet. Let her enjoy the flow and fun of the book, laughing along with the word puns and the surprise ending.

The more you read the book, the more your child will understand and appreciate the clever riddles, and how Mickey and Minnie solve them. As your child becomes more familiar with each one, stop in your reading, and encourage her to

supply the answer. Continue reading to show her that she's right!

Which riddles does your child know? Which riddles do you know? Exchange riddles with your child as you make each other laugh. You might add your own riddles to the story, too.

Read-and-Grow Activities

◆ Riddle Books

Once your child hears a funny riddle, she might not want to forget it! Help her start a riddle book to remember her riddles. Invite your child to tell you a riddle. You might start with the riddles in *The Laugh-Along Mystery*. Write the riddle on one page of a notebook. On the back of the page, write the answer. Read it back to your child, asking if you wrote it correctly. As you read, run your finger under each word so your child can associate the written words with the spoken words. When your child agrees that the riddle is correct, invite her to illustrate it. For each riddle, start a new page. Soon you will have a notebook full of riddles!

◆ Body Riddles

Play a game of charades with your child. Choose a category your child likes (for example, movie titles, book titles, book characters, food, animals, television shows, or sports). Then "tell" each other the item you are thinking about, but without speaking. You are to use body movements only. Challenge each other to figure out the answer. Remind your child that while you read words to solve a riddle, you watch body movements to play charades. Also talk about what children learned about how our bodies work from reading *Goofy Shapes Up*.

◆ What Am I Thinking?

Here's a fun way to hone your child's critical-thinking skills. Play a game of "Ask Me a Question." Sit with your child in a room. Then choose an object in that room, but don't tell her what it is. Say, "I am thinking of an object. Ask me a question to figure out what it is." You might write down the answer on a card to show your child when she answers correctly. (Review with your child the letter concepts from *Mickey's*

Alphabet Soup and the word concepts from *Mickey's World of Words* to help her read the words you have written.) Invite your child to question you as to what the mystery object is. The catch is, the questions can only have "yes" or "no" answers. For example, she could ask questions like: Is it blue?; Is it round?; Is it something I open?; Is it something you read?; Is it something you turn on?

Also let your child try to stump you. Have your child think of an item and write or draw a picture of it. Then ask her your questions. Continue as long as your child enjoys the game.

◆ Noise Riddles

Make a tape recording of sounds for your child to identify. Go around your home, and tape-record such common sounds as the running washing machine, the shower, the ding of the microwave oven, the refrigerator door opening, the vacuum cleaner, the click of the radio or TV being turned on, the flush of the toilet. Then play each sound for your child as you present her with a riddle. For example, "This makes colors bright and whites white. What is it?" (The washing machine.) Challenge your child to listen closely to the sound. Can your child tell you what it is?

◆ Riddle Walk

Go for a walk around your neighborhood with your child, and play a game of "I Spy." As you spy fun things, say, "I spy a squirrel!" "I spy the mail carrier!" Challenge your child to find the object you have spied. Make sure your child also spies fun items for you to find!

◆ Wrap It Up!

Most things for young children are riddles, for they are learning how the world works. Invite your child to continue reading *The Laugh-Along Mystery* to discover new riddles. Don't forget to reinforce the riddles she already knows. This will show your child how smart she is!

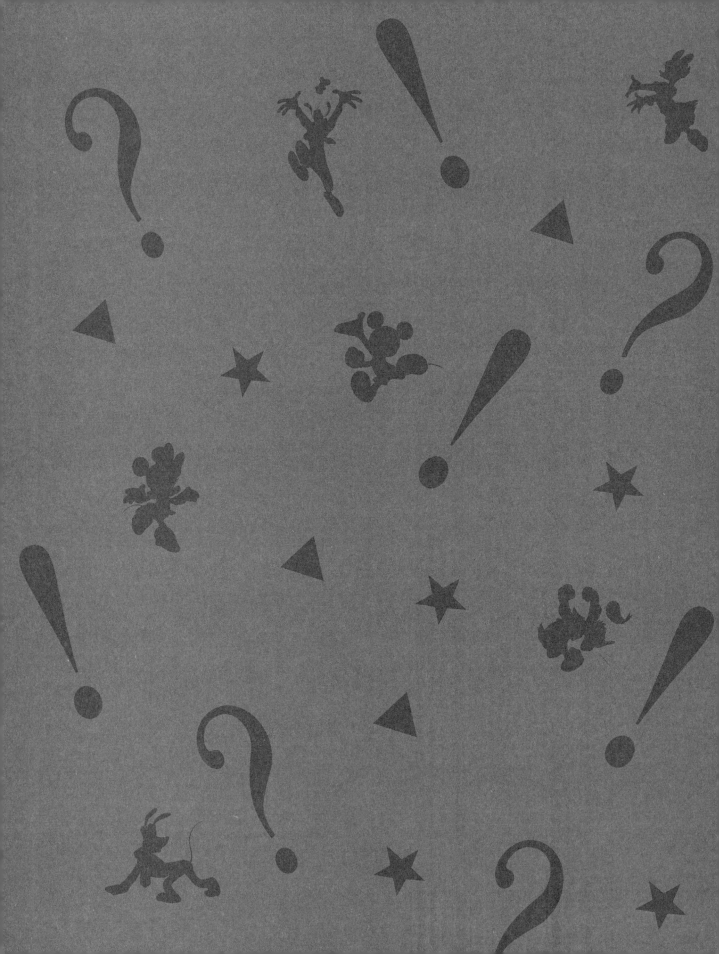